THIRTY DAYS PRAYING
The Imitation
of CHRIST
A COMPANION TO THE CLASSIC

BRIDGET HAASE, OSU

PARACLETE PRESS
BREWSTER, MASSACHUSETTS

*To the members of the Fort Square Presbyterian Church
in Quincy, Massachusetts, who, by their caring service and
compassion, show us the myriad ways of imitating Christ Jesus;
and to Edward Casey, whose prayerful self-giving in all the
ordinary circumstances of life is a witness to Christ.*

2021 First Printing

Thirty Days Praying The Imitation of Christ: *A Companion to the Classic*

Copyright © 2021 by Bridget Haase

ISBN 978-1-64060-682-1

The Paraclete Press name and logo (dove on cross) are trademarks of Paraclete Press

Library of Congress Cataloging-in-Publication Data

Names: Haase, Bridget, 1942- author.
Title: Thirty days praying the imitation of Christ : a companion to the
    original classic / Bridget Haase, OSU.
Description: Brewster, Massachusetts : Paraclete Press, 2021. | Summary:
    "Thirty days of prayer and meditation on the classic "The imitation of
    Christ", to more fully enter into daily life with Christ"-- Provided by publisher.
Identifiers: LCCN 2021011336 (print) | LCCN 2021011337 (ebook) | ISBN
    9781640606821 (trade paperback) | ISBN 9781640606838 (epub) | ISBN
    9781640606845 (pdf)
Subjects: LCSH: Imitatio Christi. | Devotional literature.
Classification: LCC BV4829 .H33 2021 (print) | LCC BV4829 (ebook) | DDC
    242--dc23
LC record available at https://lccn.loc.gov/2021011336
LC ebook record available at https://lccn.loc.gov/2021011337

10 9 8 7 6 5 4 3 2 1

Published by Paraclete Press
Brewster, Massachusetts
www.paracletepress.com

Printed in the United States of America

CONTENTS

INTRODUCTION

I n the 1970s, I was given a pocket-sized edition of *The Following of Christ*, printed in Belgium and published in St. Louis, Missouri. This treasure has gone with me to the mountains of Appalachia; to the desert of Sudan, East Africa; to the bush of Senegal, West Africa; to rural areas in Mexico; and to both Texas and Massachusetts. Now it is with me in Lewiston, Maine. This small book, prayed over by my Ursuline sister Mother Mary Mildred Dooling, is dated April 30, 1910. Sister (as we would call her now) entered the convent shortly before that day and used *The Imitation of Christ* (the book's popular name) as a spiritual guide in her religious formation.

What is most touching, I think, is the prayer Sister Mary Mildred wrote on the first blank page. She asked God to be a faithful nun "just for today." She ended her written prayer with "*Ora pro me*" (Pray for me). I am sure she took life one day at a time with no idea of what was to come over the years. She began her religious life in surrender and trust. After almost fifty-two years of self-giving service, education, and administration, Sister Mary Mildred was called to see God face-to-face on February 22, 1962.

Thank you for choosing to pray *The Imitation of Christ* for thirty days. In the interest of full disclosure, the daily selections are Sister Mary Mildred's choices. I discovered them in her fading handwriting at the end of the book. She mentions thirty days of praying the text, but certainly this can be done during the weeks of Advent, during the forty days of Lent, or extending to two and a half years (thirty months.) It is not the length of time, but the depth of absorption, that matters.

As an aside, it has been said that St. Thérèse of Lisieux treasured *The Imitation of Christ*, second only to the Bible. Legend has it that she actually knew it by heart. I find that a bit exaggerated, given the length of the book, but certainly she loved the principles which spurred her on to follow faithfully the ways of Christ in all the moments of daily life. I wonder if Sister Mildred nursed the same hopes.

Although the book I was given is a direct translation from the Latin, I have chosen to use the translation by Paraclete Press, edited by Hal M. Helms and Robert J. Edmonson of the Community of Jesus (*The Imitation of Christ* [Brewster, MA: Paraclete Press, Paraclete Essentials, Fourth Printing, 2012], with a foreword by Brother Benet Tvedten). The Introduction, the Rule of St. Augustine, and the list of scriptural references in the Appendix are "worth the price of the book," as the expression goes. Translation and text "go together like beans and cornbread," as the Appalachian saying goes. So do not shortchange the Holy Spirit or yourself, or limit your spiritual vision, by praying only the entries in the chapters of the book you are holding. Read the original, as well.

People often ask me: *Why write another book?* It is true that, for each book sold, a very small portion goes to our Infirmary fund. So, thank you for supporting our frail and ill sisters, most of whom are very elderly. But there is a more important reason—actually three. The first is that I wish to honor Sr. Mary

Mildred in the year of the sixtieth anniversary of her death. The second is that I longed to know *The Imitation of Christ* better, having been introduced to it in high school. And third, I want you, the pray-er, to come to know this spiritual treasure, discovering with me the spiritual nuggets of this classic.

I am unable to tell you how to pray, but Sr. Mary Mildred arranged her own prayerful reflection thus: the foundation of our life before God; the Incarnation, Passion, and Death of Jesus, and how they assist us in surrendering our own daily crosses and suffering as well as our daily routines; and, finally, the sweetness of eternal rest in God.

Let's look a bit more into the book's structure and author.

The Imitation of Christ (first published between 1418 and 1427 and composed in Latin) is divided into four books, each with varying numbers of chapters. The text covers helpful counsels for the spiritual life, directives for an interior life, thoughts on interior consolation, and, finally, devotion centered on the Eucharist as a key element in the spiritual life. By the seventeenth century, apart from the Bible no book had been translated into more languages. In fact, before 1650, it was printed at least 745 times, according to some popular estimates. The number of counted editions now exceeds hundreds of thousands. There are a thousand different editions preserved in the British Museum alone. Everyone can find within the text both inspiration and guidance for living well.

The authorship of *The Imitation of Christ* is generally attributed to and accepted as Thomas à Kempis (his last name was Hemerken, indicating his family's profession), who was born in 1380 in Kemp, Germany, near Dusseldorf. Both his father, a blacksmith, and his mother, a teacher, were known for their piety. At a young age, Thomas went to school in Deventer (1392–1399.) After leaving school, he journeyed to Zwolle to visit his brother Johann, who had become the prior of the Monastery of Mount St. Agnes. Thomas was quite taken with the life and in 1406 entered the monastery. He was ordained a priest in 1413.

After he became a priest, Thomas was made sub-prior and spent most of his days copying manuscripts and composing devotionals. He was also given the task of instructing those in formation (novices) and wrote four booklets between 1420 and 1427. These booklets were subsequently collected and named after the title of the first chapter of the first book, *The Imitation of Christ*.

On July 25, 1471, near Zwolle, Thomas went home to God. It is fitting that, 550 years after his death, we still devote ourselves to quietly praying this book.

The structure of this meditation book is direct. There are thirty days of prayer, and for each day there are multiple short extracts from *The Imitation of Christ*. Some themes seem to be repeated often, and perhaps Sister Mary Mildred used those themes to carve their deeper meanings in her heart. You may desire to do the same, but please do not limit yourself. Add or subtract as you follow the lead of the Holy Spirit. You may also note that the language, the meaning of words, and the spirituality seem at times to be outdated. In these moments we need to recall that *The Imitation of Christ* was written almost six centuries ago. This accounts as well for the change of pronouns and the varying lengths of chapters. Nevertheless, this book remains a classic and a pathway to everyday holiness. Only in sifting through the text will we uncover the golden nuggets of spirituality.

There is a blank section after each day's reflection to extend your prayer. It is for painting with oils, watercolors, markers, crayons, or words. You may want to doodle or write a prayer or answer the questions. Do whatever feeds your spirit and remains with you throughout these days, your retreat, your group sharing, your Eucharistic adoration, or even your finding yourself caught in traffic on your way to work or to a food pantry.

In doing so, you will be in good hands, as *The Imitation of Christ* is in yours.

Sr. Bridget Haase, OSU
Lewiston, Maine
The Feast of Pentecost

THIRTY DAYS PRAYING

The Imitation
of CHRIST

Preparation

Prayer can jumpstart our day and life, but it is never something we simply jump into. It also cannot be left to chance, as chances are the sun will set, our eyes will close, and our intention to pray will often evaporate into the darkness. Prayer requires some structure and attention, because distractions are inevitable.

This first day of this stretch of prayer is a time of getting ready to journey into the heart of Christ with a burning desire to further imitate him.

Tasks for Today

1. Fix a prayer time each day. Make this time non-negotiable, even if it means an earlier rising.
2. Choose a place that is quiet and readily available.
3. Beg for fidelity to keep these promises for the length of time decided upon.
4. Have a copy of *The Imitation of Christ* at hand so that the verses you pray over are seen in context.

Some Prayer Considerations

1. Breathe in life and exhale selfishness and self-preoccupation.
2. Check your chair and posture or your cushion and the floor space. Is it prayerful yet comfortable?
3. Enjoy your tea or coffee ahead of prayer. Try not to sip during God's time. The rest of the day is readily available to enjoy this blessing.

4. Recall God's sacred presence now and always. For Jesus promised to be with us until the end of time.

5. Let your prayer end when it ends. Set a timer, if desired.

6. Carry your thoughts throughout the day. One sentence from *The Imitation of Christ* will do. As one hot sauce ad says, "A dab will do you!"

7. Let distractions get buried in the heart of Love. Do not stew over them. Prayer is our effort; the fruits are God's.

8. Decide what you will paint or design to recall your prayer. Perhaps you are an artist in words. If so, write them down. Do not trust your memory, as the words or design may be buried in the day's routines and forgotten.

9. Thank God for the blessings and insights received. Or for the blankness that clears a space for tomorrow. All of prayer is gift, grace, and blessing.

10. Above all, pray as you can, NOT as you can't. Rise in peace and continue your day.

Pray

Come, Holy Spirit, fill the hearts of your faithful. Send forth your Spirit and we shall be re-created, and you shall renew the face of the earth. Help me to know Christ better and imitate him more devoutly in the ordinary routines and encounters of today. Amen.

Giver of Gifts

"Grant me to understand your will and to remember your many blessings with great reverence and due consideration, so that I may from now on yield you fitting thanks."

"I know and confess that I am not able to give you due thanks even for the least of your mercies."

"When I consider your majesty, its very greatness makes my spirit tremble with awe and dread."

"All that we have in our soul and body, whatever we possess outwardly or inwardly, naturally or supernaturally, are your benefits, and all show forth your bounty, mercy, and goodness, from whom we have received all good things."

"Although one may have received more, another less, nevertheless, all things are yours, and without you we cannot possess even the least of them."

"For they are greater and better who attribute less to themselves and who, in returning thanks, are more truly humble and devout."

"Those who have received fewer gifts ought not to be downcast or grieved; nor should they envy those who are enriched with greater ones. Rather let them turn their minds to you and highly praise your goodness, because you bestow your gifts so bountifully, so freely, so willingly without respect of persons."

"All things come of you, and therefore you are to be praised and blessed in all things."

"You know what is best to be given to every person, and why one has less and another more. It is not for us to reason and discuss, but for you to judge, you who know what is right for everyone."

"When we love you and acknowledge your blessings, nothing ought to give us such joy as your will in us and the good pleasure of your eternal appointing of what is to happen to us."

"With this we should be so contented and comforted that we would willingly be the least, even though others would wish to be the greatest."

"For your will and the love of your glory ought to be preferred above all things, and should comfort and please us more than all the blessings that you have given or will give us."

(BOOK 3, CHAPTER 22)

Reflect

How do I use my personal gifts for the glory of God?

In what practical ways do I offer thanks to God for the gifts bestowed upon me?

How do I handle being jealous of others' gifts?

Pray

O God, may I endeavor to give all the glory of all the good I do to you, the Giver of gifts. May I courageously offer all that I fail to do for others to your mercy. Give me the strength to do what is right and not just to do what pleases others. I offer you my gratitude and I ask that it suffice

for any shortcomings or needs that you alone know. May
I always esteem that resembling you as best I can is the
greatest gift I can offer you. Amen.

Ponder

My God-given gifts are:

*Reflect on this through words or artistry
and perhaps share.*

Imitation of Christ in Life

"It happens that many, although they often hear the Gospel of Christ, are moved by it very little because they do not have the spirit of Christ."

"Therefore, those who would fully and wholeheartedly understand the words of Christ, must endeavor to conform their lives entirely to the life of Christ."

"Great words do not make us holy and righteous; but a virtuous life makes us dear to God."

"It is better to feel contrition than to know its definition."

"If you knew the whole Bible by heart and the sayings of all the philosophers, what would this profit you without the love and grace of God?"

"It is vanity to seek perishing riches and to place trust in them. It is also vanity to look for honors and to attempt to climb to a high position."

"It is vanity to desire to live long and not to care to live well."

"Endeavor, then, to withdraw your heart for the love of things that are seen and to turn yourself to the things that are unseen."

"Seek counsel from those who are wise and who fear God."

"Do not flatter the rich or go in search of the presence of great and famous persons."

"Keep company with the simple and humble, the devout and upright. Talk with them about uplifting things."

"Desire to have close fellowship with God, his angels and saints."

"Have charity toward all, but familiarity with everyone is not advisable."

(BOOK 1, CHAPTERS 1 AND 8)

Reflect

In what ways am I living a Christ-centered life?

What changes occur in my life when I meditate on the life of Christ?

How do I practice charity toward those I do not like?

Pray

O God, let me not come before you one day having never known or loved you. Teach me to love you now and thus love you for all eternity. May my life be a surrender to your holy will. May I love you with my whole heart, soul, strength, and mind. May my life be one of charity toward all and deep humility before you and others. Amen.

Ponder

Christlike changes made in my life include:

*Reflect on this through words or artistry
and perhaps share.*

Lukewarmness

"You labor only a little now, but you will find great rest, even everlasting joy."

"If you continue to be faithful and fervent in your work, without doubt God will be faithful and liberal with you in his rewards."

"You must have a good hope of gaining the victory, but you must not think yourself secure for fear that you will grow negligent or be puffed up."

"Do now what you would do if you knew you would persevere to the end of your life. Then you would be entirely secure."

"The cost or difficulty of a conflict can deter one from spiritual progress."

"We profit most and merit greater grace where we most overcome ourselves."

"All persons do not have the same things to overcome. . . . Do not grow slack in striving to overcome the faults that most frequently offend you in others."

"If you observe anything in others worthy of rebuke, be careful not to do the same and, if at any time you have done it, strive quickly to alter your life."

"As you observe others, so also do others observe you."

"How hurtful and sad it is to see . . . others busy themselves with things that have not been committed to them."

"Those who inwardly and devoutly exercise themselves in the most blessed life and passion of our Lord will find everything there that is necessary for them so that they will have no need to seek anything beyond Jesus."

"Those who go in search of . . . ease will always be in anguish and sorrow, for one thing or another will always displease them."

"When we begin to relish God . . . we will be contented with everything that comes and in whatever may happen to us."

"When we commit ourselves to God, we will neither rejoice in having much nor be sorrowful in having little."

"Remember always your destination and that time lost never returns. Without care and vigilance, you will never acquire virtue."

"If you begin to grow lukewarm, things will begin to go poorly with you."

"But if you give yourself to zeal, you will find great peace and your labors will grow lighter by the help of God's grace and your own love of virtue."

"Those who do not avoid small faults will little by little fall into greater ones."

"You will always rejoice in the evening if you have spent the day well."

(BOOK 1, CHAPTER 25)

Reflect

What spiritual embers stir me when I am lukewarm?

When has lukewarmness given way to zeal?

How do I evaluate my days?

Pray

O good and gracious God, forgive me for criticizing
the faults of others as I excuse my spiritual laziness and
lukewarmness. It is very hard to be faithful and to attach
myself to your will when my own way demands to be
heard and fulfilled. It is simply easier to see the downfalls
of others and then, somehow, I feel better about myself.
I ask the grace to come before you as I am, weak and
fragile. I ask you to strengthen me and help me to live,
just for today, ever more intensely and devoutly for you
with no half measures. Amen.

Ponder

Ways I am lukewarm:

*Reflect on this through words or artistry
and perhaps share.*

Sorrow for Sin

"In all things, look to the end, and how you will stand before a strict judge, from whom nothing is hidden, who is not bribed with gifts, who accepts no excuses."

"Now your labor is fruitful; now your weeping is acceptable, and your sorrow is well pleasing to God and cleansing to your soul."

"It is better now to purge out our sins and cut short our vices than to reserve them to be purged away in the future."

"Be solicitous and sorrowful for your sins now, so that in the day of judgment you may have security with the blessed."

"Then the little poor cottage will be more praised than the gilded palace."

"Then enduring patience will have more might than all the power of the world."

"Then a pure and good conscience will rejoice more than learned philosophy."

"Then good works will be of greater value than many beautiful words."

"Observe now that you cannot have two joys: to delight yourself here in the world and then reign with Christ hereafter."

"All then is vanity but to love God and to serve him only."

"Those who love God with all their heart are afraid of neither death, nor punishment, nor judgment, nor hell; for perfect love gives sure access to God."

"But those who put aside the fear of God cannot long continue in good; but they will quickly run into the snares of the devil."

(BOOK 1, CHAPTER 24)

Reflect

How do my good works measure up to my word
What are my habitual sins?
What situations cause me to sin?

Pray

> O God, I know I sin by my words, especially by lying
> and gossiping. Both bring pleasant feelings and make me
> believe that I am in control of others and life itself. But then
> the illusion wears off and I have to confront the damage I
> inflicted by my words. Purify me from these sins and help
> my words to be kind, true, and just. Burn any desire to
> gossip or lie from my heart and help me to ask forgiveness
> of those whom I have hurt through my idle, untrue, and
> judgmental words. Amen.

Ponder

The reasons I lie and gossip:

*Reflect on this through words or artistry
and perhaps share.*

ayself . . . my own sins bear

myself as nothing, and think
s that I am, then your grace
will enter my heart, and all
e drowned in the depth of
...........y and perish forever."

"There you reveal to me what I am, what I have been, and where I come from. If am left to myself, I am nothing but mere weakness. But if for an instant you look on me, I am quickly made strong and filled with new joy."

"It is your love that causes all this, going before me and helping me in a multitude of necessities, guarding me from present dangers and snatching me (as I can truly say) from evils out of number."

"But by seeking you and sincerely loving you alone, I have found both myself and you, and by that love I have even more deeply reduced myself to nothing."

"Turn us to you, that we may be thankful, humble, and devout; for you are our salvation, our courage, and our strength."

"There is then no holiness, Lord, if you withdraw your hand."

"No strength helps if you cease to uphold us."

"No vigilance of our own avails if your holy watchfulness is not over us."

"If you forsake us, we sink and perish. If you comfort us, we are raised up and live."

"Where can be my confidence in my own self-conceived virtue?"

"Will the clay boast against the One who formed it?"

"Neither will those whose whole hope is firmly settled in God, be moved by the tongues of all who praise them."

"For they see well that even those who speak are themselves nothing, for they will all pass away with the sound of their words. But the truth of the Lord will endure forever."

(BOOK 3, CHAPTERS 8 AND 14)

Reflect

In what ways do I need to turn back to God?

In what ways do I seek God and not myself?

How do I feel when I am rejected or not praised?

Pray

God, in your great mercy, never allow me to attribute any gift or good to myself. Help me to realize ever more that all I have and all that I am come from you, the giver of gifts and author of any good work. Glory belongs to you alone. I am who I am before you, no more, no less. May I live only for you and by your grace. Amen.

Ponder

Praises received:

Reflect on this through words or artistry
and perhaps share.

The Inner Life

"Turn with your whole heart to the Lord . . . and your heart will find rest."

"Learn to give yourself to those things that are within, and you will see the kingdom of God come within yourself."

"For the kingdom of God is . . . peace and joy in the Holy Spirit."

"Give place, then, for Christ . . . for when you have Christ, you are rich and he alone is sufficient for you."

"He will be your provider and your faithful helper in every necessity, so you will not need to trust in mortal beings."

"People soon change and quickly fail, but Christ abides forever and stands by us firmly to the end."

"Those who are on your side today may turn against you tomorrow, and often they turn like the wind."

"Put your whole trust in God and let him be your love . . . above everything."

"He will answer for you himself and will do what is best for you."

"Here we have no lasting city. Wherever you may be, you are a stranger and a pilgrim, and you will never find perfect rest until you are fully united to Christ."

"One who views things as they are in reality, and not as they are said or thought to be, is truly wise, taught by God, rather than by other persons."

"Those who live by the Spirit quickly bring their minds back to God."

"They are not hindered by outward labor or business, which may be necessary for the time, but as things happen, they adjust to them."

"Those who are well ordered and disposed within themselves are not interested in the strange and perverse behavior of others."

"We are hindered and distracted in proportion to how much we draw outward things to ourselves."

"Nothing so defiles and entangles the human heart as the impure love of things created."

(BOOK 2, CHAPTER 1)

Reflect

In what situation do I feel I was taught by God?

When have I put my whole trust in God?

What words of Jesus am I trying to practice more intensely?

Pray

> Jesus, fill my heart with the spirit of your actions and words. Let them all be carved within me. Grant that I might surrender all the days ahead to you and become ever more yours in hope and trust. Come, live within me and help me to live only in your spirit, imitating, in season and out, your kind mercy, gentle compassion, and faithful love. Amen.

Ponder

Treasured moments of friendship with Jesus:

*Reflect on this through words or artistry
and perhaps share.*

Love of Christ

"Blessed are those who know how good it is to love Jesus."

"The love of Jesus is faithful and abiding."

"Those who embrace Jesus will stand firm in him forever."

"Love him, and hold him as your friend, for he will not forsake you when all others leave you, nor allow you to perish in the end."

"One day you will have to be separated from everyone, whether you want to or not."

"Your Beloved is of such a nature that he will allow no rival but desires to have your heart's love for himself only, and desires to reign there on his own throne."

"Whatever trust you put in people, apart from Jesus, will be little better than wasted."

"When Jesus does not speak inwardly to us, all other comfort is worth nothing; but if Jesus speaks just one word, we feel great consolation."

"Happy is the moment when Jesus calls us from tears to joy of spirit."

"How parched and hard-hearted you are without Jesus."

"What can the world confer on you without Jesus?"

"To be with Jesus is a sweet paradise."

"If Jesus is with you, no enemy can grieve or hurt you."

"They are most poor who live without Jesus and they are most rich who are dear to Jesus."

"It is a great art to know how to live with Jesus, and to know how to hold on to Jesus is great wisdom."

"Be humble and peaceable, and Jesus will be with you."

"Be devout and quiet, and Jesus will remain with you."

"You act very foolishly if you put your trust or begin to rejoice in any other."

"It is better to have the entire world against us than to have Jesus be offended with us."

"Let all be loved for Jesus's sake, but Jesus for his own sake."

"Never desire to be the object of praise or love above others, for that belongs only to God, who has none like himself."

"Resign yourself calmly to the will of God, to bear whatever comes upon you for the glory of Christ Jesus; for summer follows winter; after the night, day returns; and after the storm, there comes a great calm."

(BOOK 2, CHAPTERS 7 AND 8)

Reflect

When have I known Christ's presence in my life?
In what ways can I practice a greater closeness to Christ?
How can I be quieter and more devout?

Pray

O Jesus, so many things clamor for my time and attention each day. You bless me with twenty-four hours in each day but each one seems replete with tasks and things to do. How often I flee from prayer or make excuses not to spend time with you. Lead me by grace to love you more deeply and follow you more closely. Give me the courage to see that you are always there, waiting to embrace me.

Ponder

Things clamoring for attention:

Reflect on this through words or artistry and perhaps share.

Cross-Bearers

"Jesus has many lovers of his heavenly kingdom, but few bearers of his cross."

"He has many seekers of consolation, but few of suffering."

"He finds many companions at his feasting, but few at his fasting."

"All desire to rejoice with him; few are willing to endure anything for him."

"Many follow Jesus as far as the breaking of the bread, but few to the drinking of the cup of his passion."

"Many reverence his miracles, but few will follow the shame of his cross."

"Many love Jesus as long as no adversities come upon them."

"Many praise and bless him as long as they receive some consolation from him."

"But if Jesus hides himself and leaves them only for a brief time, they begin to complain or become overly despondent in mind."

"If we should give all we own, yet it is nothing. And if we practice great penance, still it is little. And though we may understand all knowledge, we are still far off."

"And having done all things that we know to be our duty, let us think that we have done nothing."

"Let us not think that to be great which others esteem great, but let us in truth confess ourselves to be unprofitable servants."

"Yet there is no one richer, no one freer, no one more powerful than we are, for we know how to forsake ourselves and all things, and truly put ourselves in the lowest place."

(BOOK 2, CHAPTER 11)

Reflect
What are the crosses I carry?
How can fasting extend beyond food consumption?
When does my self-interest dominate my choices?

Pray
> O God, your mercies and goodness are infinite. I deserve neither but thank you for continuing to flood my life with your unending care. Teach me to carry my crosses out of love for you and to realize that you go before me in my hour of need. You have become my Simon of Cyrene and for this I am humbly grateful. Amen.

Ponder
The crosses of selfless choices:

Reflect on this through words or artistry and perhaps share.

Challenges of Peace

"Everyone desires peace, but not everyone cares for the things that make true peace."

"Your peace will be in much patience."

"In everything take heed of yourself, what you are doing and what you are saying, and direct your whole attention to please me alone, not desiring or seeking anything apart from me."

"As for the words or deeds of others, do not judge anything rashly, or busy yourself with things not committed to your care. If you do this, it may be that you are seldom or little disturbed."

"Do not think, then, that you have found true peace if you feel no heaviness, or that all is well when you have no adversity, or that all is perfect if all things happen as you desire."

"Do not think at all highly of yourself, or account yourself to be especially beloved if you are in a state of great devotion and sweetness, for it is not in such things that a true lover of virtue is known, nor does the true progress and perfection of a person consist in these things."

"In giving yourself with all your heart to the divine will; in not seeking your own interest in either great matters or small, in time or in eternity, in this way you will be able with the same equal demeanor to give thanks in both prosperity and adversity, weighing all things in an equal balance."

(BOOK 3, CHAPTER 25)

Reflect

In what ways do I cultivate inner peace?

What is my definition of a peacemaker?

How do I achieve balance in my life in times of both adversity and prosperity?

Pray

O God, grant me the grace to know your holy will, and to depend upon it wholeheartedly. Help me to both confide in you and to abandon myself in surrender and trust. This sounds easy, God, but it is truly the challenge of my life. May I accept each moment of life and find peaceful security in your divine heart, overflowing with unconditional love for me. Amen.

Ponder

Moments of patient peace:

Reflect on this through words or artistry and perhaps share.

Things Which Bring Peace

"Make this your aim, to do the will of another rather than your own."

"Always chose to have less rather than more."

"Always seek the lower place, to be under the authority of all."

"Always desire and pray that the will of God may be wholly fulfilled in you."

"Anyone who does this enters within the borders of peace and rest."

"[This discourse] is few in words, but full in meaning and abundant in fruit."

"If I could faithfully keep it, I would not be so easily troubled."

"For as often as I feel myself disturbed and discontent, I find that I have strayed from this teaching."

"But you can do all things and always desire the progress of my soul. Increase your grace in me, so that I may be able to fulfill your words and perfect my salvation."

(BOOK 3, CHAPTER 23)

Reflect

When have I put others' desires before my own?

How do I succumb to the desire to have more and better things?

How do I subtly seek the praise of others to raise myself up?

Pray

O God, these principles are so full of meaning and abound in fruitfulness, even though they are short on words. It takes a lifetime to be faithful to these precepts, but I want to carry them in the backpack of my life. I ask that I draw strength from them when I feel weak and barren, nourishment when I am hungry, and refreshment when I am parched and burdened. Amen.

Ponder

Ways to desire less:

Reflect on this through words or artistry and perhaps share.

DAY 12
Service

"You have shown me the sweetness of your love, that when I had no being, you made me, and when I was far astray from you, you brought me back again to serve you; and you entreat me to love you."

"Is it any great thing that I should serve you whom every creature is bound to serve?"

"See, everything that I have, and everything with which I do you service are yours."

"And, yet, on the other hand, it is you who serve me rather than I, you."

"You yourself have stooped to serve humankind, and have promised to give yourself to us."

"Would that I could at least for one day do you some worthy service!"

"Truly you are worthy of all honor, all service, and praise forever."

"Grant me, most merciful Lord, the favor of supplying what is lacking in me."

"It is a great honor and a great glory to serve you."

"How pleasant and delightful is the service of God, by which we are made truly free and holy."

(BOOK 3, CHAPTER 10)

Reflect

How do I feel about serving through menial tasks?
How do I serve God by serving others?
What do I feel is lacking in me?

Pray

O God, erase within me the vain complacency that swells my pride and convinces me that it is I who do good. Actually, it is only my Christian responsibility to assist others and it is the Holy Spirit who enlightens me and spurs me on with courage and conviction. Grant me the grace to serve joyfully, not counting the cost or measuring the success of my efforts. Help me to know deep in my being that there is always more I could do and that, in the end having done all I can, I remain an unprofitable servant. Teach me the spiritual art of praising you, for without your divine assistance, I can do nothing. Amen.

Ponder

Ways to serve:

Reflect on this through words or artistry and perhaps share.

Moderation

"You must conform your desires in all things to my good pleasure, and you should not be a lover of yourself, but be earnestly zealous that my will be done."

"Various desires often enflame you and drive you violently headlong; consider whether you are being moved by your self-interest rather than for my honor."

"If I am your motivation, you will be well contented with whatever I ordain. But if there is lurking in you any self-seeking, this will hinder you and weigh you down."

"Not every impulse that seems good is to be heeded immediately, nor, on the other hand, is every contrary feeling at once to be avoided."

"It is well to check yourself at times, even in good desires and endeavors, so that you will not through too much eagerness become distracted in mind, or by lack of self-control create a scandal to others; or again, facing opposition or resistance by others, become suddenly confounded and so fall."

"[You are to be] pleased with plain and simple things and . . . not murmur at any inconvenience."

(BOOK 3, CHAPTER 11)

Reflect

In what ideas do I need moderation?

What are some of my good desires?

How can I take pleasure in simple things?

Pray

God, I seek only your will for me but often have no clue what it is. Teach me moderation when I pipe dream or get carried away about how I could change the world. Help me to love simple things, like sunrises and juicy strawberries, and never to murmur when the sun grows hot or the snow mounds freeze. I deeply desire to accept inconvenience as a source of patient moderation. Amen.

Ponder

Cherished simple things:

*Reflect on this through words or artistry
and perhaps share.*

True Lovers of God

"At a little adversity or opposition, you abandon what you have undertaken and too greedily seek some outward consolation."

"Valiant and faithful lovers of God stand fast in temptations and do not yield to the crafty persuasions of the enemy. As I please them in prosperity, so I do not displease them in adversity."

"Prudent lovers do not consider the gift as much as they do the love of the Giver."

"Noble lovers do not rest in the gift, but in me above every gift."

"All is not lost, then, if you sometimes feel less devotion to me and to my saints than you would like to feel."

"That good and sweet affection which you sometimes feel is the effect of present grace, a sort of foretaste of your heavenly home; but it is not good to lean too much on such comforts, for they come and go."

"Do not let strange fancies trouble you, on whatever subject they may crowd into your mind. Keep your resolution with courage and persevere in your upright intention toward God."

"Know that the ancient foe, the devil, will try by every means to hinder your desire to do good and to divert you from every religious exercise, if he can."

"Do not believe or listen to him, no matter how often he sets his traps of deceit to ensnare you."

"Fight like a good soldier. And if through your weakness of character you sometimes fall, rise up with greater strength than before, trusting in my more abundant grace. But guard yourself beforehand against complacency and pride."

"Let the fall of the proud who presume on their own strength serve as a warning to you to keep you ever humble."

(BOOK 3, CHAPTER 6)

Reflect

In what ways am I valiant and wise?

What are my good works?

How am I tempted?

Pray

O God, many times I hesitate to proclaim you as the source of all my gifts. I lack the courage to do this as I do not want to be gossiped about as being "over the top" or laughed at because I am seen as a religious fanatic! Many times, I have palpably felt your presence and for this I am grateful. Keep me from falling into the trap of denial or, at least, of a wish-washy acknowledgment of your grace in my life. Keep me humble but help me to be ever more valiant and wise. Amen.

Ponder
Bold proclamations:

*Reflect on this through words or artistry
and perhaps share.*

Difficulties in Life and in Prayer

"Cloudless day of eternity, which no light darkens, but which is perpetually lightened by the supreme truth! Ever joyful day, ever secure and never changing."

"Would that day had dawned and that all these things of time had come to an end!"

"To the saints indeed it shines, resplendent with everlasting brightness; but to those who are pilgrims on the earth, only as far off and as through a dim mirror."

"The days of this life are short and evil, full of sorrow and anguish."

"When will I have steady peace, undisturbed and secure peace, peace within and peace without, peace assured in every way."

"Comfort my exile, lessen the intensity of my sorrow, for my whole desire sighs after you."

"I long to enjoy you in my inmost soul, but I cannot lay hold on you."

"I desire to cling to heavenly things, but temporal things and unmortified passions weigh me down."

"As a result, unhappy that I am, I fight with myself and have become a burden to myself, while the spirit makes an attempt to be above."

"Pardon me and in your mercy forgive me, as often as in prayer I think about anything besides you."

"I truly confess that I am inclined to yield to many distractions."

"For often I am not there, where I stand or sit, but rather I am where my thoughts carry me."

"If I love heaven, I willingly think on heavenly things."

"If I love the Spirit, I delight to think on spiritual things."

"For whatever I love, of that I willingly speak and hear, and carry home with me the mental image of it."

(BOOK 3, CHAPTER 48)

Reflect

What are the crosses I carry?

In what ways is God a mystery to me?

What personal deficiencies can I surrender to God?

Pray

O God, I ask your merciful forgiveness as I seek earthly things even in my prayer. Distractions of power and prestige overcome me even as I long to be attentive in your presence. My thoughts often carry me to the realm of dreams and to things that pass away. Where my treasure is, there will be my heart. So, I beg you to purify my being so as to think on eternal values. Amen.

Ponder
Some eternal values:

*Reflect on this through words or artistry
and perhaps share.*

Wise Conduct

"You must endeavor with all diligence in every place, in every action, and in all your outward business to keep yourself inwardly free and be master of yourself. Be sure that all these things are under you and that you are not under them."

"You must be ruler and master of your own actions, not a servant or a hired hand."

"Rather, you should be as a free person . . . for they stand above present things and contemplate eternal things. They look on the passing things with the left eye, and with the right they see the things of heaven."

"If you stand steadfast in everything and do not judge what you see and hear by the outward appearance or with a worldly eye, but enter at once in every circumstance like Moses into the tabernacle to ask counsel of the Lord, you will often hear the divine word and come out instructed in many present and future things."

"You should . . . flee to the secret tabernacle of your heart and very earnestly implore divine help."

"Always commit your cause to me, and I will take care of it in due time."

"Mortal beings often struggle mightily for something they desire, and when they obtain it, they begin to feel another way; for human affections do not long continue directed on the same thing, but rather shift from one thing to another."

"It is no small gain, then, to forsake yourself even in the smallest thing."

"Watch and pray (says the Lord) so that you do not enter into temptation."

(BOOK 3, CHAPTERS 38 AND 39)

Reflect

What helps do I have to avoid evaluating by appearances?
What responsibilities or worries do I commit to Christ?
In what ways can my actions make me a hired hand?

Pray

O God, you care for all things and love me without any conditions. It is a mystery to me, then, that I do not trust your divine providence to assist me in times of need. I foolishly think that I can do things myself or that I have no need of your help. Nothing can be farther from the truth. With you, all things are possible but, without You, I can do nothing. You are always there for me, in season and out. Deepen my faith in your daily care, for you know what I need and will provide. Amen.

Ponder
Personal divine instructions:

*Reflect on this through words or artistry
and perhaps share.*

The Way of the Cross

"For those who now gladly and willingly hear and follow the word of the cross will not then be afraid that they will hear the sentence of everlasting damnation."

"This sign of the cross will appear in heaven when the Lord comes in judgment."

"Then all the servants of the cross, who in their lifetime conformed themselves to the Crucified One, will draw near to Christ the Judge with great boldness."

"Why do you dread to take up the cross, since it is the very way to the kingdom of heaven?"

"Take up your cross, therefore, and follow Jesus, and you will go into everlasting life. He went before you bearing his own cross and died for you upon the cross, so that you might also bear your cross and that you should be ready to die on the cross."

"There is no other way to life and true inward peace, except the way of the holy cross and of daily self-denial."

"Go where you will, seek whatever you will, you will not find a higher way above or a safer way below, than the way of the holy cross."

"You will sometimes feel forsaken by God, at other times you will be troubled by your neighbors, and what is more, you will sometimes be a burden to yourself."

"No one feels the suffering of Jesus so intensely as one who has suffered similar things."

"Turn upward, turn downward, turn outward, turn inward, you will find the cross everywhere, so you always need patience if you would have inward peace and win a lasting crown."

"If you bear the cross cheerfully, it will bear you and bring you to your desired goal, where there will be an end of suffering, even though this cannot be here."

"It is not our way to bear the cross, to love the cross . . . to flee honors, to suffer being insulted . . . to endure all adversities and losses, and to desire no prosperity in this world."

"But if you trust in the Lord, strength will be given you from heaven, and the world . . . will be made subject to your command."

"If you are armed with faith and signed with the cross of Christ, you will not fear your enemy the devil."

"For surely if there had been anything better and more useful than suffering for the health of the human soul, Christ would certainly have shown it by word and example."

(BOOK 2, CHAPTER 12)

Reflect

In what ways do I boldly and cheerfully accept my daily crosses?
How am I a trouble to myself?
How can I help others carry their cross?

Pray

O God, although I know that the only way to eternal life is through the cross, I resent it when the cross enters my life. I know in my head that it is the path to heaven and that you go before me. Yet, I recoil from the stringent demands the cross makes on my life. Permeate my life with a faith that allows me to cheerfully and gratefully embrace whatever comes my way. I ask for patience, strength, and courage to change my attitude toward the cross in my life and to trust completely that you will support me when I begin to sink under its weight and demands. Amen.

Ponder

My attitudes toward life crosses:

Reflect on this through words or artistry and perhaps share.

True Glory

"What have we done for you that you should grant us your grace?"

"Unless you help me and inwardly instruct me, I will become altogether lukewarm and dissolute."

"But, Lord, you are always the same and you endure forever. You are always good, just, and holy, doing all things well, justly, and in holiness. You always dispose everything with wisdom."

"Yet, when it pleases you, things quickly become better with me when you stretch forth your helping hand. For you can help me alone, without human aid, and you can so strengthen me that my heart will no longer be attracted toward other objects but will be turned and will rest in you alone."

"You are my glory; you are the joy of my heart."

"To you alone be honor, acclaim, praise, and glory for ever and ever."

(BOOK 3, CHAPTER 40)

Reflect
How have I succumbed to a vain display of success?
In what ways is God's glory magnified in me?
When does my heart rest in God?

Pray
O God, may you alone be praised and glorified in all that I do. May I always yield to your plan for me and learn

to rest in you, for you are humble of heart. Thank you for the gift, grace, and blessing of my life. We both know that I can claim nothing but my weaknesses, for they are truly mine. I ask for the grace to always believe in your unconditional love and to surrender to your holy will in all that I do. May you be the joy of my heart as I render praise for all that you accomplish in and through me. To you be glory and honor forever. Amen.

Ponder

Divine blessings:

Reflect on this through words or artistry and perhaps share.

Friendship and Learning

"If you set your peace in any person, you will always be unstable and never content."

"Your regard for your friend ought always to be grounded in me, and you are to love that friend for my sake, whoever that person is that you think well of, and who is very dear to you in this life."

"Without me, no friendship is firm or will long endure; nor is that love pure and true that is not held together by me."

"No matter how small a thing is, if you love it inordinately, it holds you back from the highest and corrupts you."

"Do not let the fair and subtle words of other persons move you. For the kingdom of God is not in word, but in power. Give attention to my words, because they kindle hearts and enlighten minds; they bring awareness of guilt and carry with them many a consolation."

"Never read the Word in order to appear more learned or wise."

"I am the One who teaches knowledge to humankind, and I bestow to little ones clearer understanding than can be taught by persons."

"The time will come when Christ, the Teacher of teachers, the Lord of angels, will appear to hear the lessons of all—that is, to examine the consciences of everyone."

"I am the One who in an instant elevates a humble mind, so that people will understand more of eternal truth than if they had studied ten years in the schools."

"I teach without noise of words, without confusion of opinions, without desire for honors, without the wrangling of arguments."

"I am the One who teaches mortals . . . to seek eternal things, to relish eternal things, to flee honors, to endure scandals, to place all hope in me, to desire nothing out of me, to love me ardently above all things."

"To some I speak common, plain things; to others, special things. To some I gently show myself in signs and figures, while to some I reveal mysteries in much light."

"A book has only one voice, but it does not instruct everyone alike. For I am the teacher of truth within, I am the searcher of the heart, the discerner of the thoughts, the mover of actions, distributing to every person as I deem fit."

(BOOK 3, CHAPTERS 42, 43)

Reflect

What graces do my friends offer me?

What can I learn from my teacher, Christ?

How do I put into action God's words and call to me?

Pray

O God, please spare me from the muddle of my own words, which I use to reinforce my opinions or inner biases. Help me to truly listen to your Word, especially when I am tempted to glaze over or ignore it because I feel disturbed or uncomfortable. Thank you for sending me true and sincere friends. Bless them and keep them in your heart each and every day. Keep me there as well, just as I am, often weak and filled with doubts and insecurities. As you love my friends, as I love them, so much more do You love me. Lord, I believe. Increase my faith. Amen.

Ponder

Lessons from my friends:

Reflect on this through words or artistry and perhaps share.

God's Word

"The words I have spoken to you are spirit and life and cannot be fully comprehended by human understanding."

"[God is] to be heard in silence and received with great humility and great affection of the heart."

"I taught the prophets from the beginning [says the Lord], yet I do not cease to speak to every creature even to this day; but many are hardened and are deaf to my voice."

"The world promises temporal things of small value, and yet it is served with great eagerness. I promise things that are most high and eternal, and yet human hearts remain slow and dull."

"People undertake a long journey for a little reward; for eternal life many will hardly lift one foot from the ground."

"They seek after the most pitiable reward; for a single penny sometimes there is shameful contention. For a slight promise or a little trifle people do not hesitate to toil day and night."

"But what a deep pity this is! For an unchangeable good, for a reward beyond all price, for the highest honor, for glory that has no end, they begrudge the slightest fatigue."

"What I have promised, I will give, and what I have said, I will fulfill, if only a person will remain faithful in my love even to the end."

"[Lord,] remember your mercies, and fill my heart with your grace, for you do not will that your works should be in vain."

"How can I bear the miseries of this life unless you give me strength by your mercy and grace in it?"

"Teach me, Lord, to do your will. Teach me to walk worthily and humbly before you. For you are my wisdom; you know me in truth, and you knew me before the world was made and long before I was born into the world."

(BOOK 3, CHAPTER 3)

Reflect

In what ways are the promises of God fulfilled for me?
How do I put silence in my life to listen to God?
When have I intentionally put all my trust in God?

Pray

O God, sometimes I am so hard of hearing that I need you to sear your words in my heart. Help me to receive them in reverence and in humility. Quiet my mind and my life with all the noisy worries that claim my attention. Fix my heart upon heaven and upon the things that really matter, for one day with you is worth a thousand days with the things of earth. Amen.

Ponder
Mysterious words of God:

*Reflect on this through words or artistry
and perhaps share.*

Effects of Divine Love

"Because I am as yet weak in love and imperfect in virtue, I need your strength and consolation. Visit me often, then, and instruct me with holy discipline."

"Love is a great good, a great good indeed; by itself it makes everything light that is burdensome and it makes the rough places smooth."

"It bears a burden without being burdened, and it makes all that is bitter sweet and pleasant."

"The ennobling love of Jesus impels us to great things and stirs us up to desire greater perfection."

"Love tends upward and refuses to be held down by even the lowest and humblest things."

"Nothing is sweeter than love, nothing stronger, nothing higher, nothing broader, nothing more pleasant, nothing fuller or better in heaven or on earth, because love is born of God and cannot rest finally in anything lower than God."

"Love does not feel any burden, is not concerned with how much labor it must do, attempts what is beyond its strength, and does not plead any excuse that something is impossible, for it thinks it can and may do all things."

"Love is watchful, and sleeping, is not in a slothful state. Weary, it is not exhausted; pressed, it is not constrained; alarmed, it is not terrified. Like a lively flame or a burning torch, it forces its way upward and safely triumphs."

"Love is swift, sincere, pious, pleasant, and strong; it is patient, faithful, longsuffering, strong, and never self-seeking."

"For wherever we are self-seeking, there we fall from love."

"Love is circumspect, humble, and upright, not soft, not fickle, not intent on vain things. It is sober, chaste, steady, quiet, keeping guard over all the senses."

"To God, [love] is thankful and devout, ever trusting and hoping always in him, even when it does not sense God's presence, for no one lives in love without some sorrow and pain."

"Those who love, ought to embrace willingly all that is hard and distasteful for the sake of their Beloved, and must not turn away from him on account of any adversity that may happen to them."

(BOOK 3, CHAPTER 5)

Reflect

How did I cope when love was a faint ember?
In times of adversity how do I trust God?
What are the qualities of my love for God?

Pray

God, I must admit that my fire of love for you does go out. Adversity overtakes and overwhelms me, and I wonder if you notice or even care. To make matters worse, I feel guilty that I do not trust you. I long to persevere in my love for you and surrender to your will, but there are so many excuses I make for my laxity. In a nutshell, more often than not, I do not embrace these trials willingly but fight them and you. But you always know and accept that. My love dwindles; yours, never. I believe. Help my unbelief in life's off seasons. Amen.

Ponder

What I have learned from people who love me:

*Reflect on this through words or artistry
and perhaps share.*

Referring All Things to God

"If you seek yourself in anything as the end of your work, you wither away in yourself and become dry and barren."

"I desire that you refer all things to me first of all, for I have given everything to you."

"From me the small and the great, the rich and the poor, draw the water of life as from a living fountain. If you freely serve me you will receive grace upon grace."

"Do not ascribe any goodness to yourself or attribute goodness to any person, but ascribe all goodness to God, without whom humanity has nothing."

"I have given all, and I will have everything returned to me again."

"If heavenly grace and true love come into you, there will be no envy or narrowness of heart, and self-love will not rule in you."

"The love of God overcomes all things and expands all the powers of the soul."

"If you are truly wise, you will never rejoice except in me, and you will hope in me alone; for none is good but God alone, who is honored above all things, and in all things to be blessed."

(BOOK 3, CHAPTER 9)

Reflect

What does it mean to me to draw the water of life as from a living fountain?

When have I noticed a narrowness of heart inside me?

In what ways do I render praise and thanks to God?

Pray

> Dear God, I thank you for your patience with me when I think that I am the one who has accomplished any good. How happy I would be if I could say that my works are directed to you and your glory! But that would be untrue. I ask the blessing to realize that all that I do comes from you alone. As with the great St. Paul, I can glory in nothing, except in my weakness, which makes me equal to all humanity and saved by you. Amen.

Ponder

Powers of my soul:

Reflect on this through words or artistry and perhaps share.

True Opinion of Self

"All persons naturally desire knowledge, but what good is knowledge without the fear of God?"

"Surely a humble peasant who serves God is better than a proud philosopher who, neglecting his own soul, occupies himself in studying the course of the stars."

"If I understood everything in the world and did not have divine love, what would it avail me in the sight of God, who will judge me according to my deeds?"

"Learned persons are anxious to appear learned to others, and to be called wise."

"Many words do not comfort or satisfy the soul, but a good life comforts the heart, and a clean conscience gives great confidence toward God."

"The more you know and the better you understand, the more strictly you will be judged, unless your life is also more holy."

"Do not be elated in your own mind, then, because of any ability or knowledge you may possess, but rather let the knowledge given you make you more humble and cautious."

"If you think that you understand and know much, know also that there are many more things you do not know."

"Why would you set yourself above others, since there are many more learned and more skillful in the Scripture than you are?"

"The highest and most profitable learning is a true knowledge and humble opinion of oneself."

"If you should see another openly sin or commit some grievous offense, you should still not think yourself better because of it; for you do not know how long you will be able to stand."

"We are all weak and frail; but you should regard no one frailer than yourself."

(Book 1, Chapter 2)

Reflect

How do I dream about a search for deeper knowledge?

In what ways can I be peaceful about knowing what I do not know, about accepting my weakness and sinfulness?

What aids do I have to help me think kindly of those who are difficult?

Pray

Good and gracious God, I desire to be honest with you. I love to be considered learned and wise, in life and all its branches. Somehow, I manage to sweep under the rug the admission that there are many things I do not know and concentrate on flaunting what I do know. Perhaps this is a human quality, but it is certainly not humility. Help me to accept and own my sins and personal weakness without blaming others for my lapses. Temptation is real and I often fall into it. You know it and so do I. Amen.

Ponder
Personal weaknesses:

Reflect on this through words or artistry and perhaps share.

Benefit of Adversities

"It is good that we sometimes have troubles and crosses, for they often make us think about ourselves, and consider that we are here in a state of exile and ought not to place our trust in any worldly thing."

"It is good that we are sometimes opposed, and that others think ill of us or misunderstand us, even though we have done and intended well."

"These things often help us attain humility and defend us from vain pride, for we are more inclined to resort to God for our inward witness when we are outwardly rejected and dismissed as contemptible and unworthy by others, and no credit is given us."

"We should therefore so settle ourselves in God that we do not rely on the reassurances of other persons."

"Perfect security and peace cannot be found in this world."

(BOOK 1, CHAPTER 12)

Reflect
When do I feel rejected?
In what ways do I rely on God?
How do I handle anxiety?

Pray

O God, I ask for divine support in all the trials and troubles that come to me. In these times, never let my love of neighbor or fidelity to you weaken. Help me to use all the temptations and adversities that come my way to deepen my trust in your powerful assistance and ongoing care. Amen.

Ponder

Moments of anxiety:

Reflect on this through words or artistry and perhaps share.

Love of Solitude and Silence

"Seek a convenient time to search your own conscience and think often about the loving kindness of God."

"Do not read for curiosity's sake or simply to fill up the time, but read such things as will stir your heart to devotion."

"If you will refrain from idle talk and idly running about, from listening to gossip and rumors, you will find ample time for meditation on good things."

"No one can safely speak but those who would gladly be silent."

"No one can safely command but those who have learned to obey."

"No one can truly rejoice but those whose heart witnesses that they have a clean conscience."

"In silence and in stillness the devout soul advances and learns the mysteries of the Holy Scriptures."

"It is better for you to be unknown and to take heed for your own soul than to work miracles in the world."

"Close the door behind you and call to yourself Jesus your Beloved."

(BOOK 1, CHAPTER 20)

Reflect

When is it difficult to place hope in God?

How do I find solitude in the midst of busy days, household chores, and family demands?

In what ways do I strive to deepen my prayer life?

Pray

O God, thank you for manifesting the joy and beauty of life and giving me an appreciation for both. Granted, there are many books I have not read, but enlighten me so that I choose those that inspire and increase my devotion. I desire to love stillness, finding it in the bustle and noise of life. Help me to stop and pray, for time spent with you is not a waste of my day or my energy. Amen.

Ponder

Inspiring and devotional books:

Reflect on this through words or artistry and perhaps share.

Attaining Peace and Growth in Grace

"We would enjoy much peace if we did not occupy ourselves with the words and activities of others, and with things that are of no concern to us."

"How can persons remain long in peace who intrude into the affairs of others, who look for occasions to travel about, and who seldom give serious thought to themselves?"

"Blessed are the single-hearted, for they will enjoy much peace."

"We are led too much by our feelings, and we are too concerned about transitory things."

"We seldom overcome one fault perfectly. We have too little eagerness to grow spiritually every day, and so we remain cold and lukewarm."

"When some small difficulty arises, we are quickly downcast in spirit and turn to people for consolation."

"If we tried like brave persons to stand in this spiritual battle, surely we would experience the help of God from heaven."

"If we rely only on some outward observances for progress in our spiritual life, our devotion will quickly run out."

"But let us lay the axe to the root, so that being freed from our passions, we may find rest for our souls."

"If we would root out one fault every year, we would soon become mature."

"Our fervor and our progress should increase daily, but it is now considered a great thing if we can retain even some part of our initial zeal."

"It is a hard matter to give up evil habits, but it is even harder to go against our own will."

"If you cannot overcome the small and easy things, how will you overcome the harder ones?"

"If only you knew how much inward peace to yourself and joy to others your good outward manner would obtain, I think you would take more care about your spiritual growth."

(BOOK 1, CHAPTER 11)

Reflect
In what situations do I intrude in the affairs of others?
What faults do I need divine assistance to root out?
In what ways do I care for my spiritual growth?

Pray
O God, is it not self-centered to think that by eliminating one fault I will grow in grace? Teach me that holiness is to live in fidelity to life's demands of the present moment. I beg for a clarity of inner sight and the courage to be faithful to my daily responsibilities. Keep me from dreaming about doing big things for you and, in the process, miss the ordinary things that help me grow in grace and lead to true holiness. Maybe a fault I need to eradicate is the notion of desiring to be in control of every situation and event in my life. Is not surrender to *what is* and *what will be* a growth in grace? Amen.

Ponder
One fault to eradicate:

*Reflect on this through words or artistry
and perhaps share.*

Enduring Hard Things

"Do not let yourself be dismayed by the labors you have undertaken for me [Christ], neither let yourself be cast down because of any trying experiences that come to you. But let my promises strengthen and comfort you in all events."

"I am well able to reward you above all measure and degree."

"You will not labor long here, nor always be grieved with sorrows."

"Wait a little while and you will see a speedy end to all your troubles."

"There will come an hour when all toil and tumult will cease. Little and brief is all that passes away with time."

"Do what you have to do with all your might."

"Write, read, sing, sigh, keep silence, pray; bear crosses courageously; life everlasting is worthy of all these conflicts and even greater things than they."

"Peace will come in a day known to the Lord. It will not be day and night as in this life, but eternal day, with infinite brightness, abiding peace, and unending rest."

"Should not all labors gladly be endured for the everlasting joys?"

"It is no small matter to lose or gain the kingdom of God."

"Lift up your face therefore to heaven. Look! I and all my saints with me, who have had great conflicts in this world, now rejoice, are comforted, are now secure, are now at rest.

And they will remain with me for all eternity in the kingdom
of my Father."

(BOOK 3, CHAPTER 47)

Reflect

What promises to Christ bring me hope?

Why are hard things worth enduring?

What effort do I put into my daily routines?

Pray

God, I am quite poor at enduring hard things. To be
honest, hard things often overcome me and drain the
hope from me. It is hope that the world needs, and I
know that, if I am to imitate Christ, I am to bring this
hope to others. Grant me the grace to be courageous in
small things without hope of a reward and use this to
show others the way and so to imitate Christ. Amen.

Ponder
Hard things inspiring hope:

*Reflect on this through words or artistry
and perhaps share.*

Rewards Promised to Those Who Fight Against Sin

"When you find yourself longing for everlasting, complete happiness given you from above, and long to depart out of the tent of this body so that you may see my glory that is without any shadow due to change, open your heart wide and drink in this holy inspiration with all the desire of your soul."

"Give fullest thanks to the heavenly Goodness that treats you with such voluntary descent from its place on high, visiting you mercifully, stirring you up fervently, powerfully lifting you up so that you will not fall down to earthly things by your own weight."

"The fire often glows, but the flame does not ascend upward without smoke."

"In the same way, the desires of some persons are ablaze toward heavenly things, but they are not free from the temptations of worldly affection."

"Do not ask for what is delightful and profitable to you, but for what is acceptable to me and is for my honor."

"For if you judge rightly, you ought to prefer and follow my will rather than your own desire or anything whatever that is to be desired."

"You long now to enjoy the glorious liberty of the children of God. Now you would delight in the everlasting habitations, your heavenly home, full of joy. But that hour is not yet present. There still remains another time, a time of fighting, labor, and trial."

"You must still be tried on this earth and tested in many things."

"Take courage, then, and be valiant in doing things that are repugnant to nature as well as in suffering them."

"You must often do what you do not want to do and leave undone what you would prefer to do."

"At this, nature will sometimes complain and grumble, and it is no small thing if you bear it all in silence."

"But consider . . . the fruit of these labors, how quickly they will end, and their exceedingly great reward, and you will not grudge to bear them. Rather you will have the solace to strengthen your patience."

"I will give you glory instead of the reproach you endured here, the garment of praise instead of sorrow, and instead of the lowest place, a kingly crown for all eternity."

"Let this be your constant desire, that whether in life or death, God may always be glorified in you."

(BOOK 3, CHAPTER 49)

Reflect

What sins do I fight against?

In what ways am I afraid to die?

What is heaven like to me?

Pray

Good and gracious God, you flood my life with mercy. It is totally undeserved. You love me unconditionally. It is the gift of your grace, freely bestowed, that helps me fight against sin. I have no idea why I fear death and facing you who are only filled with love for me. I guess it is because I just do not handle mystery well and do not want to relinquish control. Amen.

Ponder

Situations in which to fight sin:

Reflect on this through words or artistry and perhaps share.

Resting in God

"Above all things and in all things, my soul, rest in the Lord, for he is the eternal rest of all his saints."

"Grant me . . . to rest in you above all created things, above all health and beauty, above all glory and honor, above all dignity and power, above all knowledge and subtlety, above all riches and talent, above all joy and gladness, above all fame and praise, above all sweetness and consolation, above all hope and promise, above all merit and desire."

"For surely my heart cannot truly rest or be entirely satisfied unless it rests in you and rises above all gifts, and all other created things whatsoever."

"When will it be fully granted me to consider the quietness of mind and to see how sweet you are, my Lord God?"

"Come, come! For without you there will be no glad day or hour, for you are my gladness and without you my table is barren and empty."

"Let others seek instead of you whatever they please; nothing else that I seek, nothing that I will seek can please me, but you, my God, my hope, my eternal salvation."

"Blessed are you, therefore, Lord, that you have showed this goodness to me after the multitude of your mercies."

"Your works are good, your judgments are true, and by your providence all things are governed."

"Therefore, to you, Wisdom of the Father, be everlasting praise and glory. Let my mouth, my soul, and all your creatures praise and bless you together."

(BOOK 3, CHAPTER 21)

Reflect

In what ways can I rest in God?

How is resting in God not a passive, do-nothing approach to the pain and needs of others?

What richness does God bring to my life each day?

Pray

O God, there is such a fine line between resting in you and tirelessly working to make this world a better place by alleviating the needs of others. Erase in me the tendency I have to rashly judge those who take a stand for justice and then decide that they need to learn how to rest. Perhaps this comes from my own guilt or laziness. Enlighten me, quicken my spirit, so that my days are neither wasted nor rushed with self-absorbed, frenetic activity. Amen.

Ponder

Ways to rest in God:

*Reflect on this through words or artistry
and perhaps share.*

The Sweetness of God's Love

"'My God and my all.' To those who understand this word, enough is said; and to repeat it again and again is pleasant to those who love you."

"You give tranquility to the heart, great peace, and pleasing joy."

"You cause us to take delight in all things and to praise you in everything, nor is anything able to bring lasting pleasure without you. If anything is pleasant and gracious, it is because your grace is present and it is seasoned with your wisdom."

"[Those who love and rest in the Divine] have a relish for God, and whatever good is found in created things, they refer it all to the praise of their Maker."

"Even so, there is a great difference between the sweetness of the Creator and the creature, of eternity and time, of light made and light unmade."

"Purify, gladden, enlighten, and quicken my spirit . . . so that it may cling fast to you with an abundance of joy."

"Show your greatness, I entreat you, and let your right hand be glorified, for I have no other hope or refuge but you, Lord my God."

(BOOK 3, CHAPTER 34)

Reflect

How is God really "my all"?

In what ways does the sweetness of God permeate my life?

How do I witness in a practical way to the sweetness of God?

Pray

Sweet God, it is so easy to glorify and praise you when all is going smoothly. I attribute this to you, but, deep down, I feel I am in control of my life. When the unexpected happens, I question not just your presence but also your sweetness. Aid me to truly love you, and to see you in every person, in every event in life. Let me stretch out my hand to yours and know that, no matter what, your hand holds me in sweetness and in love. Together it is onward and upward. Amen.

Ponder

Moments of God's sweetness:

*Reflect on this through words or artistry
and perhaps share.*

CONCLUSION

This manuscript was all ready to send to the editor, the gracious and understanding Jon Sweeney of Paraclete Press. However, I must have pressed an incorrect key as everything disappeared. I was reduced to frustrating tears, as months of work were gone. But, trusting in advice given to me ages ago by John Brande, I picked myself up, dusted myself off, and began again. Accidentally deleting everything was a blessing in disguise. In starting over, I became a pray-er and not just a writer or gleaner.

This is my hope for you, the pray-er. Become a living example of the spiritual values of *The Imitation of Christ*. If you are reading this, perhaps you could ask yourself, *Did I give this book and a solid translation of the classic itself a read-through or a pray-through?* If, in answering this, you choose the latter, then Sr. Mary Mildred is happy—and so am I and so is the editorial staff at Paraclete Press! The hours spent in writing, editing, and producing this book have borne fruit.

May you be a true imitator of Christ, like the members of the Fort Square Church in Quincy, Massachusetts, and Mr. Edward Casey. All, quietly hidden and without fanfare, continue Christ's divine work upon this earth. They are graces for us all!

ACKNOWLEDGMENTS

In loving and thankful memory of my Ursuline sister Mary Mildred Dooling, OSU, who imitated Christ by the love and devotion she brought both to her religious community and to her high school students; and in the honored and grateful memory of her nephew, John Dooling, a man of indomitable faith, who died during the writing of this manuscript. John was the beloved and devoted husband of Ann and the father of five children.

ABOUT PARACLETE PRESS

Who We Are

As the publishing arm of the Community of Jesus, Paraclete Press presents a full expression of Christian belief and practice—from Catholic to Evangelical, from Protestant to Orthodox, reflecting the ecumenical charism of the Community and its dedication to sacred music, the fine arts, and the written word. We publish books, recordings, sheet music, and video/DVDs that nourish the vibrant life of the church and its people.

What We Are Doing

BOOKS | PARACLETE PRESS BOOKS show the richness and depth of what it means to be Christian. While Benedictine spirituality is at the heart of who we are and all that we do, our books reflect the Christian experience across many cultures, time periods, and houses of worship.

We have many series, including *Paraclete Essentials*; *Raven* (fiction); *Iron Pen* (poetry); *Paraclete Giants*; for children and adults, *All God's Creatures*, books about animals and faith; and *San Damiano Books*, focusing on Franciscan spirituality. Others include *Voices from the Monastery* (men and women monastics writing about living a spiritual life today), *Active Prayer*, and new for young readers: *The Pope's Cat*. We also specialize in gift books for children on the occasions of Baptism and First Communion, as well as other important times in a child's life, and books that bring creativity and liveliness to any adult spiritual life.

The MOUNT TABOR BOOKS series focuses on the arts and literature as well as liturgical worship and spirituality; it was created in conjunction with the Mount Tabor Ecumenical Centre for Art and Spirituality in Barga, Italy.

MUSIC | PARACLETE PRESS DISTRIBUTES RECORDINGS of the internationally acclaimed choir *Gloriæ Dei Cantores*, the *Gloriæ Dei Cantores Schola*, and the other instrumental artists of the *Arts Empowering Life Foundation*.

PARACLETE PRESS IS THE EXCLUSIVE NORTH AMERICAN DISTRIBUTOR for the Gregorian chant recordings from St. Peter's Abbey in Solesmes, France. Paraclete also carries all of the Solesmes chant publications for Mass and the Divine Office, as well as their academic research publications.

In addition, PARACLETE PRESS SHEET MUSIC publishes the work of today's finest composers of sacred choral music, annually reviewing over 1,000 works and releasing between 40 and 60 works for both choir and organ.

VIDEO | Our video/DVDs offer spiritual help, healing, and biblical guidance for a broad range of life issues including grief and loss, marriage, forgiveness, facing death, understanding suicide, bullying, addictions, Alzheimer's, and Christian formation.

Learn more about us at our website:
www.paracletepress.com
or phone us toll-free at 1.800.451.5006

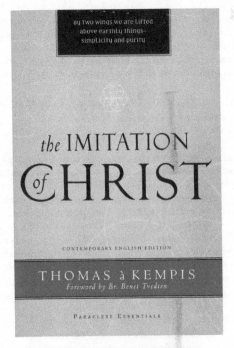